TAKAPUNA BEACH

A neglected community asset

Semisi Pone

BSc, MSc (Hons)

Cover picture: The 'trenches' being dug up by storm water as it empties onto the beach. There are several of these trenches across Takapuna Beach.

CONTENT

Introduction

Introduction

If you take a brisk walk along the length of Takapuna Beach, it will take about 30 minutes. It is one of my favorite spots for a stroll to 'clear the cobwebs' as a writer. The clean sea air and view, waves crashing on the sand and cries of sea birds are very good therapeutic stimulants for the senses.

This book is not a scientific study but an opinion based on the 'photo evidence' and what is going on at Takapuna Beach. I have been visiting and swimming at Takapuna Beach since 1980 and I can definitely say it is not as clean as it was before. It is an excellent beach, probably one of the best in Auckland and New Zealand, but it is not managed properly and protected for the future.

I take my children and grand-children there and I feel really bad because of the state of the 'cleanliness of the beach'. There are warning signs there that the storm water flowing into the beach is polluted, millions of liters of polluted water during every storm empty into the sea turning it into a 'muddy color' and sediment wash up on the sand and turn it from white to brown in color. I cannot believe that nothing is being done to improve the situation.

This book presents the 'photo evidence' with some suggestions as to how I believe it should be done. This presentation is designed to 'get the ball rolling'. Many articles and letters in the Northshore Times, over the years, have been lamenting the 'disgusting' state of the beach but no one is willing to do anything. Even the Auckland City Council does not have any plans to clean it as far as I can tell from my brief discussion with the Takapuna-Devonport Local Board.

Our Project Revival Charity Trust(Inc) have already presented a proposal to the Takapuna-Devonport Local Board to clean the beach 'all year round'. We can use some of our unemployed youth, adults and volunteers to clean the beach as one of our 'job creation activities'. I have also sent the Mayor of Auckland, His Excellency Len Brown a copy of our proposal.

I would like to take my grand-children there when the place is a bit cleaner. I love to watch them and listen to their little voices as they giggle, laugh and get excited over their sand castles or swimming and playing with each other.

I believe that more should be done. There should be a 'catchment pipe' about one meter in diameter running along the length of the beach 'hugging the land' and collecting the run off. Then from that catchment pipe another 3-4 pipes about half a meter in diameter runs out to sea for a kilometer or so where the storm water flows out into the open ocean and disperse. That will ensure no polluted water enters the sand or beach area where our children and grand-children play. It will be very expensive to fund such a project but it is the only way. All the pipes should be buried and out of sight or the sight of them will be 'visual pollution' to local and visitors alike.

The Takapuna Beach area is already popular with bars and restaurants moving into the immediate area, I am sure that at some time in the future it will become a very important 'seaside focal point of economic activities' like restaurants and bars as more and more residential houses turns into commercial outlets. More tourists will visit the area and boost the local economy with their cash.

There is, at least one children's playground already sprouting up on the beach.   I am sure other commercial activity will come.

Any plan for the future should take these developments into account.

Semisi Pone
BSc, MSc (Hons)
Chief Executive
Project Revival Charity Trust (inc)

Chapter 1. Takapuna Beach Background

Takapuna Beach is an excellent community asset, with lots of sand and space, located on the waterfront of the Auckland suburb of Takapuna on the Northshore. It takes about 30 minutes to walk from one end to the other, quickly, or up to 40 minutes at a leisurely pace. It is fairly big and a popular spot for families to bring their children and grand-children for picnics or swim there on hot days during summer.

Many new restaurants and bars have sprung up around the beach area in the last 10 years and I am sure more will come as the residential houses turn into commercial ventures.

Tourism in New Zealand is booming with increased travellers from China and Asia coming to the Northshore and spending their cash there. It is to be expected that such a well located beach will have development potential in the future.

The problem at the moment is that the storm water system fom the shopping area of Takapuna empties on to the beach. It has turned the sand from white to brown and the sea from turquoise to muddy. It is not a desirable result. If the storm water can be dispersed out in the open ocean, the sea can clean the beach by washing away all the dirt.

There is also an unacceptable amount of both organic and inorganic rubbish accumulating on the beach. Grass and weeds start to grow on this accumulated rubbish as can be seen from the pictures.

The only solution is to rake up all this rubbish and take them to the rubbish dump. Organic rubbish can be composted and sold or used for community projects.

Chapter 2. The Current Council Plan

From our discussions with the Takapuna-Devonport Local Board during the Project Revival Charity Trust (Inc) presentation I made, on the 24th of May, 2016, regarding cleaning of the beach; there is no current plan to clean the beach or improve the storm water drainage system.

This is an unacceptable situation and should be improved with some plans to tackle the problem as a matter of priority.

The problems of global warming and sea level rise are attributed to man made pollution. New Zealand is a signatory to global treaties to reduce national carbon output as one of the measures to mitigate problems with global warming. At the same time, beaches and natural areas are neglected. This double standard should be 'corrected' as the problem of the environment is not restricted to carbon emission only. Disposal of polluted storm water and beach rubbish is also part of the 'overall' picture and should be addressed as soon as possible.

Chapter 3. Public/Community Asset

Takapuna Beach is one of the best and most popular beaches in all of Auckland. When I first visited the beach in 1980, I remember being blinded by the shiny sand at mid-day. It was so white and clean it reflected the light from the mid-day sunshine which was hard to look at without blinking or narrowing ones eyelids to block out most of the glare. I remember it was very clean without any rubbish in sight.

Now, 36 years later the sand is brown to black from the organic sediment and other pollution. The sea which was much cleaner is now muddy colored most of the time.

Figure 1. Runoff seeping off this stone wall blackens the sand

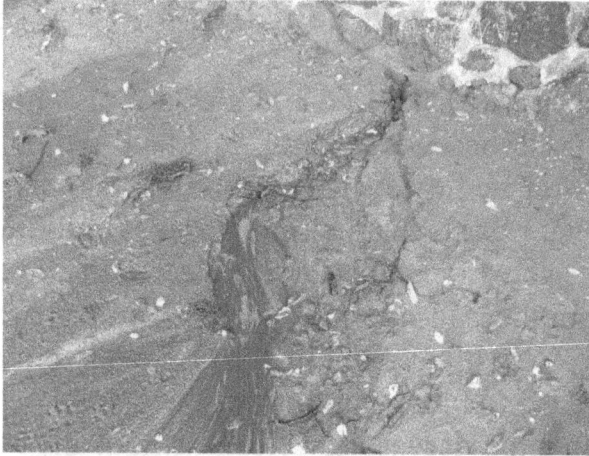

Figure 2. Rivulets of water from this wall shows how the black colored pollution spreads

Figure 3. In comparison, here is a picture of what the clean sand should look like.

A public asset or amenity is for the people and visitors to use in as good and natural a condition as possible. In this case, Takapuna Beach is clearly polluted and children, or anybody, should not be swimming there.

Figure 4. There are several signs near storm water pipes warning kids not to swim here because it is polluted!

If the puddles around the storm water pipes are polluted then surely the run off to the sea is also polluted!

Chapter 4. Inorganic rubbish on Takapuna Beach

The following pictures speak for themselves. There are hundreds or even thousands of pieces of inorganic rubbish on Takapuna Beach although it is not very obvious.

Plastic is well known to cause poisoning of marine life who eats them. I have seen pictures of birds, in wild life articles about pollution, with their crops full of plastic!

Figure 5. This is a piece of paper or plastic with organic rubbish like leaves and twigs

Figure 6. Two pieces of timber with organic rubbish

Figure 7. A discarded jandal among organic rubbish

Figure 8. A piece of tissue in the grass

Figure 9. A piece of timber

Figure 10. A discarded 'Snicker Chocolate' wrapping

Figure 11. A piece of metal on the beach

Figure 12. A piece of plastic

Figure 13. A plastic bottle

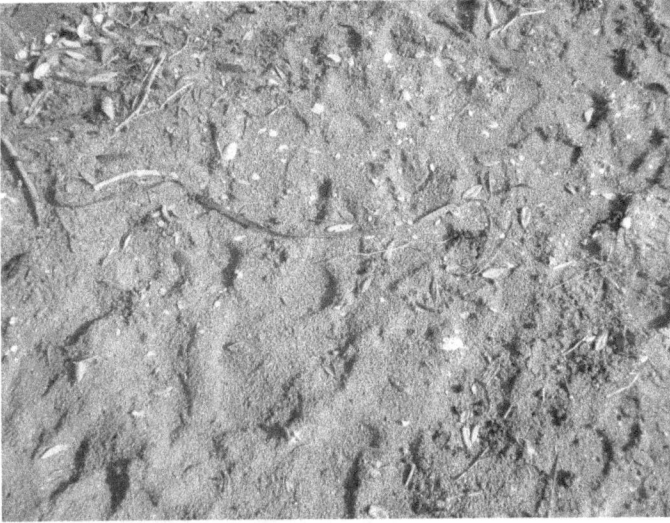

Figure 14. A piece of plastic rope

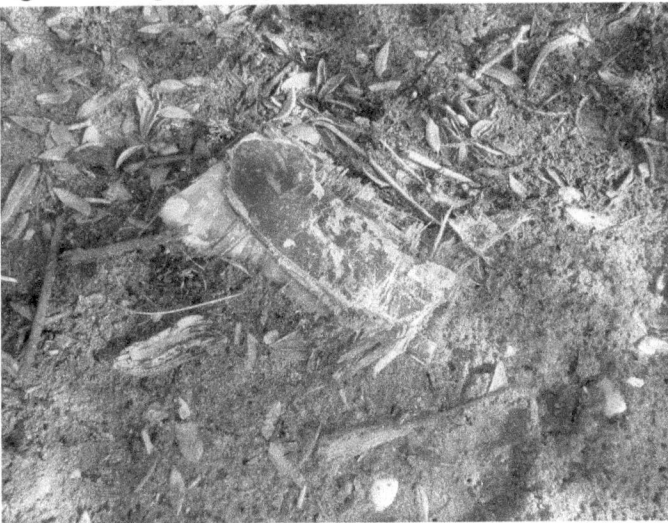

Figure 15. A piece of plywood

Figure 16. A worn out rugby ball among seaweed overgrown with grass

Figure 17. A piece of plastic or paper among organic rubbish

Figure 18. A piece of plastic and organic rubbish

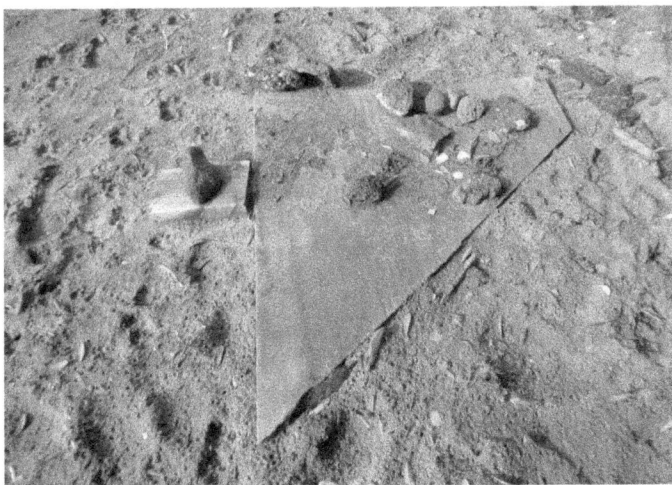

Figure 19. A large piece of plywood

Figure 20. Discarded clothes can also be found on the beach

As mentioned before the inorganic rubbish like plastic, papers and timber are small but numerous. It is not very obvious but can fill several bags once collected. These inorganic rubbish look 'fresh' and recently added.

There may others buried under the sand and grass.

Chapter 5. Organic rubbish on Takapuna Beach

It is arguable that kelp and seaweed brought by storms on to the beach, broken branches and leaves can break down on their own, naturally. The problem is that the organic compost adds to the 'blackened' sand and it is already very clear from the collected pictures.

Figure 21. Dried seaweed and tree leaves. Note the 'dark' color of the sand

Figure 22. Organic rubbish on beach

Figure 23. More organic rubbish.

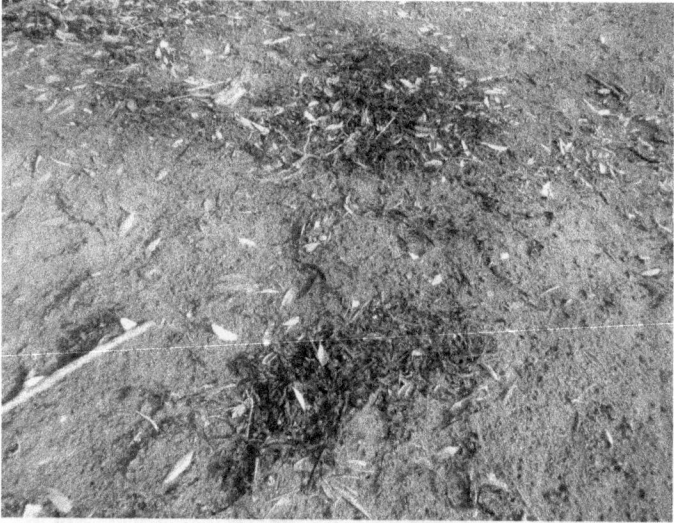

Figure 24. Organic rubbish consisting of seaweed and leaves from surrounding trees. Note dark color of the sand.

Figure 25. A broken storm water pipe

Figure 26. Unsightly debris on the sand and overgrown with grass. Note 'dirty' soil colored look of the sand.

Figure 27. A fresh piece of seaweed. Note the clean color of the sand at the water's edge

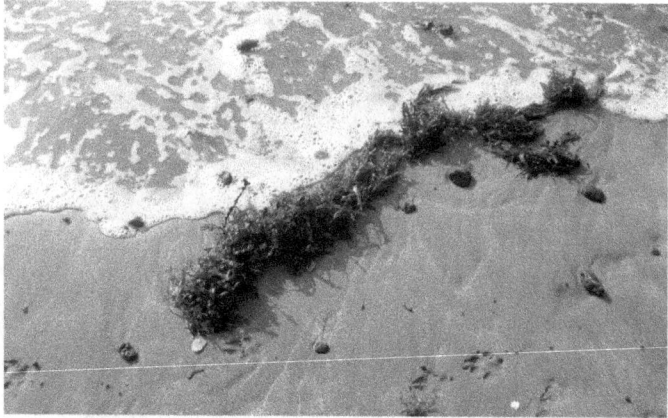

Figure 28. A fresh piece of seaweed brought in by the tide. Note 'brownish' color of the sand.

Figure 29. Another fresh piece of seaweed. Note the 'clean' color of the sand.

Figure 30. A typical sight after storms. In some cases the sand is completely covered with kelp and other seaweed.

Figure 31. The seaweed accumulates at the edge of the beach where it is 'covered' with grass growth.

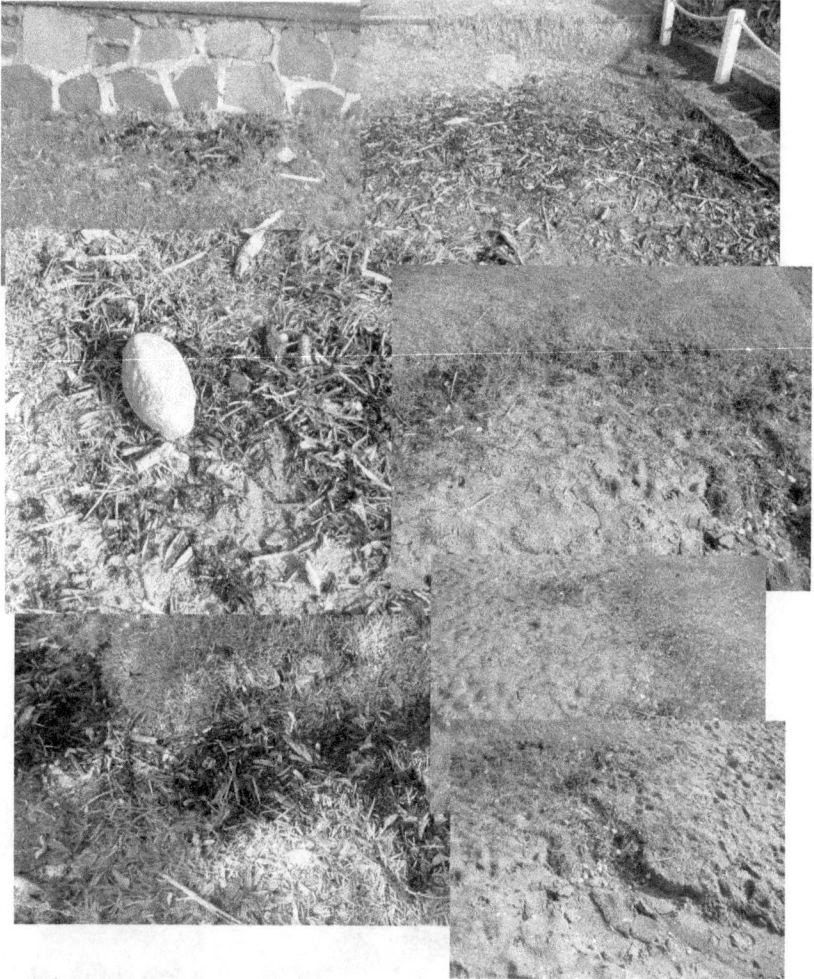

Figure 32. Accumulating
organic rubbish overgrown with grass at the edge of
the beach.

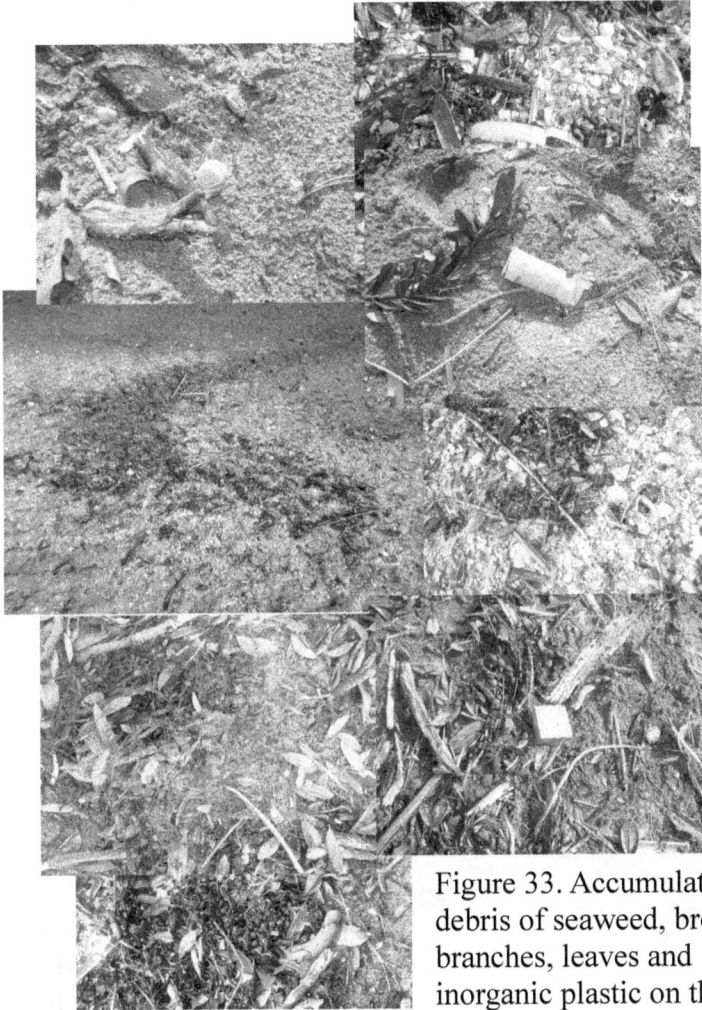

Figure 33. Accumulating debris of seaweed, broken branches, leaves and inorganic plastic on the sand.

Figure 34. Images showing clear evidence of the 'dirt' or sediment discoloring the sand in many places across Takapuna Beach.

Figure 35. More rubbish and debris

From all the pictures presented so far, there is only one conclusion; the beach needs to be cleaned of all the debris and rubbish. One could argue it is natural, but it is not. The natural state of the beach was a white sandy beach with cleaner water. On a sunny day the glare of the sand, as it reflects the sunlight, hurts most people's eyes. Now the dirt is absorbing all of the sunlight and there is no 'glare' at all.

Figure 36. A pile of seaweed has been sitting on the beach for so long that grass is growing over it.

Figure 37. A children's playground on the beach. Note the 'dirty color' of the sand.

Chapter 6. Stormwater pipes flowing onto the beach

There are many storm water pipes emptying onto the beach. It is quite clear that is the major cause of the 'muddy' appearance of the water and discolored 'dirty' appearance of the sand.

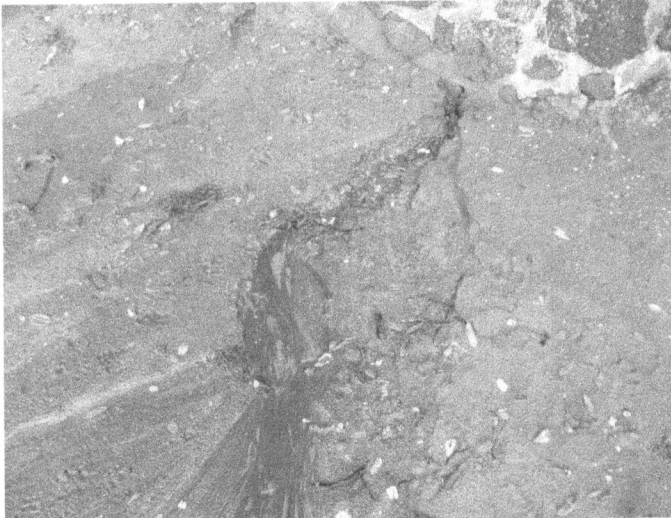

Figure 38. This 'black' sand is the result of pollution. Whatever it is, it cannot be good for the beach.

Figure 39. This 'trench' was dug up by water from the stormwater pipe below (Figure 40).

Figure 40. The biggest storm water pipe on Takapuna Beach 'digs a trench' up to 3 feet deep on the sand (Fig.39).

Figure 41. Stormwater pipes digs some 'impressive' sized trenches on the sand.

Figure 42. Stormwater pipes can bring debris and rubbish off the land onto the beach.

Chapter 7. Warnings of contaminated water

Figure 43. This storm water pipe has a sign beside it that says, 'Hey kids.... Don't swim or play here. This water is polluted!'

If it is polluted why are people still allowed to swim in the sea? There are millions of liters of polluted water from land that flows into the sea during every storm.

Figure 44. This storm water pipe also has a sign warning that the water is polluted!

During every rain storm there are millions of litres of water emptying on to Takapuna Beach from all the storm water pipes shown in the pictures. If there is a warning its polluted water, why are children still allowed to swim there?

Comment on marine species and pollution indicators.

Marine life in any area of the sea or beach is a good indicator of the health of the sea in that area.

During this 'quick survey', there were no marine animals/species seen except the ubiquitous sand flea. There are hundreds of them under the piles of rubbish. Is that an indicator of the health of the beach?

An over abundance of one species and the lack of others could be a sign of pollution.

There were no shellfish (sea snails), crabs or hermit crabs seen. Pipi and cockles were found on Takapuna Beach in the past. If they are gone, could it be a sign of pollution or over fishing?

As far as I know there are no shellfish gatherers at Takapuna Beach.

Chapter 8. What can be done?

First solution.

I have already mentioned our Trust is proposing to clean up the beach using our unemployed youth, adults and volunteers. The proposal document was presented to the Takapuna-Devonport Local Board. We simply rake up the rubbish and take them to the rubbish dump. Organic rubbish like seaweed and leaves from the beach trees can be composted.

Second Solution.

There need to be a catchment pipe, perhaps one meter in diameter, running the length of the beach 'hugging' the land to collect all the water off the storm water pipes, streets and land 'run off'. From this catchment pipe 3-4 smaller pipes, perhaps, half a meter in diameter, running out to sea for one kilometer where the storm water will be dispersed into the open ocean so it does not cause any problems on the beach. Our children and grand-children play and swim on the beach. It will be very irresponsible of the Auckland City Council not to clean up the beach and improve the current storm water drainage system for our children and grand-children's sake.

After all, what are we going to give the children in the future? A beach full of polluted water with conditions so unhygienic that marine species are disappearing off the beach? Is that something you want your children and grand-children to inherit from you?

It would be better to fix the beach for the kids, as a top priority, while other 'less urgent' costs like new tunnels and so on relegated down the priority list.

PROJECT REVIVAL CHARITY TRUST (INC)
BOOK, ART, AND MUSIC EXHIBITION
...the purpose is to inspire our youth
...the theme is excellence in education

The PRCT is holding a Book, Art and Music exhibition at the Methodist Hall, 139 Queens Road, Northcote Point on Saturday the 18 of June, 10am-5pm.
The profits will be used to print free books for our reading programme. The books will be given to the kids and youth of Northcote (Tonar St, Lake Rd, Fraser Ave, Richardson Pl and Cadness St, as Christmas presents. Last year (2015) we gave 60 copies of THE DREAMTIME STORIES by Semisi Pone as Christmas Presents for our kids and youth.

Contact Semisi Pone, Chief Executive, PRCT (Inc)
Ph. 02102695563,
email; rainbowenterprises7@gmail.com

....200 books for Christmas 2016...

This project will cost $NZ4,000. If you are interested in helping with our reading programme, you can donate a book for one of our kids ($NZ20 each) this year. Bank Account, Project Revival Charity Trust (Inc), Account 389016022741100.
Contact Semisi Pone, Chief Executive, PRCT (Inc) on 02102695563 or rainbowenterprises7@gmail.com

Notes on the author.

Semisi Pone graduated with a BSc in 1985 and MSc (Hons) in 1989 from the University of Auckland. He has worked for the Ministry of Agriculture (Tonga) as a Plant Pathologist/Senior Virologist (June, 1985-March, 1992), University of the South Pacific as a Fellow in Tissue Culture (April 1992-May, 1993), South Pacific Commission as the Plant Protection Advisor (June 1993-May 1996). During his time with SPC, he was also Co-ordinator for the Plant Protection Service with several multi-million dollar projects; including being manager of the $NZ5 million SPC/EU Pacific Plant Protection Project. He was also an expert on Phytosanitary Measures/Biosecurity for the Food and Agriculture Organization of the United Nations (Rome, Italy) for 7 years but only completed 3 years when he migrated to New Zealand in 1996.

He was also a part-time lecturer in first year biology and second year ecology at the University of 'Atenisi in Tonga (1991), with experience from studies of the Auckland seashore/marine biology at stage 2 in Auckland University.

In Auckland, Semisi has been involved with many businesses since 1996 and became a full time writer since 2011. He has self-published more than 100 books and ebooks which are on sale online at amazon.com, wheelers.co.nz , apple.com and blurb.com

Semisi also works for the Project Revival Charity Trust (Inc) as a volunteer/trustee/executive to promote its work programme using his experience (2013-2016).

Attachment 1. Proposal for the cleanup of Takapuna Beach

PROJECT REVIVAL CHARITY TRUST (INC)
PRESENTATION
On the clean-up of Takapuna Beach

By Semisi Pone
BSc, MSc (Hons)
Chief Executive/Trustee
Ph:02102695563

Email:rainbowenterprises7@gmail.com

7.00 pm, Tuesday 24, 2016.
Takapuna-Devonport Board Meeting
Council Chambers
1 The Strand
TAKAPUNA

TRUST INFORMATION.

The PRCT was established by a group of Tongan elders in Northcote and incorporated on the 18 of June 2013 as a response to the Tongan youth 'law and order' problems in Northcote mainly Tonar St, Cadness St, Lake Rd, Fraser Avenue, Richardson Place and the immediate area. Prior to 2013 more than 10 of the Tongan youth and young men were jailed for various preventable offenses. After the PRCT was established and many discussions and activities held, we believe that the Tongan youth 'law and order' problem in Northcote is, largely, gone. There may be isolated 'flare-ups' but they are not very common. The main charitable purpose is the promotion of education through reading.

In 2015, the PRCT printed 60 copies of the children's book THE DREAMTIME STORIES by Semisi Pone and gave them to Northcote families with kids as Christmas presents.We hope to give away 200 books as Christmas presents for our kids this year (2016).We have started a small business for training of the youth. It is still being organised. We hope to add the Takapuna clean-up to our youth job creation activities. There are many other traditional and group activities like sports being planned. The Deed of Trust and Principles and Purposes of the PRCT are available from the Companies Office.

The Trust earns some money from book sales, sausage sizzles and donations which are minimal and requires more funds for its programmes. The Trust is organising a book, art and music exhibition this June (June 18, 10am-5pm, Methodist Hall, 139 Queen Street, Northcote Pt) to promote local writers, artists and composers and to inspire our youth and children. The current Trustees are Mr Semisi Pone sr, self-employed; BSc, MSc (Hons), Auckland University, (Chief Executive); Mrs Pinomi Vaitohi, housewife ; Mrs Lavinia Pone Pule BBS (AUT), housewife; Mr Semisi Pone jr, business owner. We are still in discussion with the Charities Commission regarding registration.

1. The Proposal

The PRCT propose to takeover the daily cleanup of Takapuna Beach as part of its Youth Job Creation Programme.

Background.

I have enjoyed swimming and walking on Takapuna Beach for more than 20 years. I believe it is one of the best Community Assets on the Northshore. My children and grand-children also enjoy swimming and playing on Takapuna Beach.

Over the past few years, I have read many reports, articles and letters in the Northshore Times about the deteriorating state of Takapuna Beach and the lack of a 'cleanup team' to take care of the beach. I do agree, I have noticed that the beach is not as clean as it was 20-30 years ago. The sand does not look as white and there are more rubbish like plastic, cans, bottles and organic debris like seaweed, mainly kelp, on the beach on most days of the year.

Our proposal is very simple. The PRCT tries to help our youth and children with promoting of reading by providing free reading books and also activities like job creation. We propose to clean up Takapuna Beach for 2 hours every afternoon/evening. That is 14 hours a week. We also propose an emergency arrangement for

removing 'large amounts of kelp and rubbish' after storms and both costs to be included as part of the Takapuna-Devonport Board budget. It is a very cheap way to look after this Community Asset for all the visitors and regular fans of Takapuna Beach. The waterfront is becoming very popular with bars and restaurants so it is a timely setup for the future.

This arrangement will allow the PRCT to rotate the youth and kids from Northcote in this highly valuable experience activity to gain some self-confidence and self-esteem. The youth and kids who are unemployed or who need a part time job will be asked to help and will be paid a part time wage by the PRCT. The kids gain some valuable experience and pocket money and Takapuna Beach will be much cleaner and presentable to all locals and visitors alike. Kids will also get references and support from the Trust to get a full time job as they move on to other careers.

Proposed Budget

1. 14 hours a week (2 hours a day) @ $25 per hour
$350.00

2. Consumables per week
   - plastic bags for rubbish collection @$5/25
   $5.00
   -petrol @ $70
   $70.00
   -disposable gloves @$10/box

$10.00
-disposal at dump (based on one load per week/7days) $150.00

Total weekly costs
$585.00

3. One off consumables/equipment
-rakes x 6 @$10 each
$60.00
-6 bright colored hi-viz @ $5 each
$30.00
-6 printed caps @ $30 each
$180.00
-6 gumboots@$20 each
$120.00
-2 wheelbarrows @$200 each
$400.00
-2dustpans and brooms @$10 each
$20.00
-6x heavy duty gloves @$7.00 each
$42.00

One off consumable/equipment one off cost
$852.00

4. Emergency kelp/seaweed/rubbish cleanup after storms
Four people x 4 hours = 16 hours @ $25 per hour
$400.00
-$40 petrol (based on one full tank of diesel)
$40.00

-$140 disposal(based on one truckload)
$140.00
-$10 bags (50 large heavy duty bags)
$10.00
-$70 (2 tonne truck hire)x2 hours
$140.00

Payout as per emergency
$730.00
(On requests)

5. One off vehicle cost

-purchase of secondhand vehicle/ute
$5,000

Budget Comments

This budget is a very simple and workable 'cheap'
budget to permanently have a team cleaning
Takapuna Beach as a Community Asset for the
Northshore, Auckland and the rest of New Zealand
and tourists alike. After the initial 'one off' cost of
$5852 the ongoing cost is only $585 a week and $730
per emergency, after storms.The emergency fund is
only paid when there is a storm and the beach is
covered with seaweed, kelp and other rubbish, like
broken branches and leaves, as has happened often in
the past during winter months when we need extra
hands to clean the beach.

Depending on how the council works the funds can

be provided on a monthly or 3 monthly instalments into the Trust account. The cost of emergency funds can be paid when required provided it can be done on the day of the emergency so workers can be paid after the cleanup is done.

This project is an excellent fundraiser for the Trust to fund its Christmas presents and other costs by savings from labor costs . This year (2016) the Trust aim to provide 200 free copies of a novel printed from USA as Christmas presents for the youth and kids of Northcote, for example. This is part of our reading programme promotion. It will also give our Northcote kids, who cannot find employment or who need a part-time job somewhere to work part-time for the Trust and feel proud about what they do for their community as well as themselves.

Staff Supervision

All staff/volunteer work on the Takapuna Beach clean-up will be supervised by myself, Semisi Pone (Chief Executive) or delegated to a trained senior/older person to supervise if I am not available.

My Background

I have a BSc (1985) and MSc (1989) from the University of Auckland. I have worked for the Ministry of Agriculture, Tonga, at senior level for 6 years. I was a Fellow at the University of the South Pacific, Agriculture Campus, Apia, Samoa for 1.5

years and Plant Protection Advisor/Co-ordinator for the South Pacific Commission Plant Protection Service in Fiji for 3 years. I was also a member of the experts on Biosecurity/Phytosanitary Measures at the Food and Agriculture Organisation, United Nations (Rome) for 7 years (only completed 3 years as I migrated to New Zealand in June, 1996). I was the Manager of the SPC/EU $NZ5 million Pacific Plant Protection Project during my time with SPC and was involved with many other multi-million dollar projects as the Co-ordinator of the SPC-PPS.

I have been involved with many businesses in New Zealand since June, 1996. Since 2011, I have been a full time writer with more than 100 books and ebooks on sale in New Zealand and online. I volunteer to work for the Trust on a part-time basis, like the other Trustees, when required. I also operate a 'Lawnmowing and Gardening Buisness' which we hope to use as a model to train the kids and for volunteer work like the Takapuna Beach clean-up. It is still a small operation and is not ready for any trainees yet.

I have done some studies of the seashore in parts of Auckland and marine biology in year two Bachelor of Science at the University of Auckland so I am aware of the sensitive nature of the beach ecosystem and I will try to produce some information on the Takapuna Beach marinelife over time as we become familiar with them which will be useful for tourists and visitors interested in Marine Biology and Beach Ecosystems.

Other Comments

The Trustees hope to begin sports activities for our youth soon when funds permit, like tennis and sevens rugby, for example. The Netball North Harbour and Takapuna Rugby Club are very close to our area and the kids will love having sports activity at those excellent facilities.

The Trust has introduced other programmes like our online 'reading books' in blurb.com where kids can read story books with a Pacific theme and look at our picture books from Tonga and New Zealand with 200-300 pages to view. We have been experimenting with an online school for the New Zealand born Tongan kids where they can learn topics like Tongan traditions and culture, Traditional song compositions and also Tongan language children's stories. Our online resources are/will be available to all New Zealanders.